Elon Musk:

199 Best Quotes from the Great Entrepreneur – Tesla, SpaceX, Exciting Future, Money, Failure and Success

(Powerful Lessons from the Extraordinary People Book 1)

edited by
Olivia Longray

Cover photo by Steve Jurvetson on Flickr

Copyright © 2017, 2020 Olivia Longray
All rights reserved.

Revised and Updated Edition 2020
First Published in 2017

ISBN-13: 978-1977691576
ISBN-10: 1977691579

"No, I don't ever give up. I'd have to be dead or completely incapacitated."

—Elon Musk

Contents

Introduction 5
Part 1: LIFE LESSONS 7
    Meaning of Life 7
    Childhood & Upbringing 10
    Education 13
    Money & Debts 16
    Personal Life 19
    Engineering & Design 21
    Politics & Democracy 23
    Mentality of a Samurai 25
Part 2: INCREDIBLE PROJECTS 27
    Tesla 27
    SpaceX 31
    Solar Power 34
    Autonomous Cars 36
    Journey to Mars 39
    Exciting Future 43
    Hyperloop 45
    Democratization of AI Technology 47
    Simulated Reality 51
Part 3: SUCCESS LESSONS 53
    Why Failure is Fine 53
    How to Deal with Fear 56
    Listen to Negative Feedback 57
    How to Get New Ideas 59
    Innovative Thinking 60
    Persistence & Patience 61

    Work Like Crazy 62

    The Biggest Mistake 65

    Make Something Valuable to People 66

    Train Yourself to Think Differently 67

    Tell the Truth 69

Part 4: BRILLIANT ADVICE FOR ENTREPRENEURS 70

    How to Create a Successful Company 70

    Advice on Raising Capital 74

    Qualities of Prosperous Entrepreneurs 75

    Hire Smart and Creative People 76

    What a Brand Is 78

    Don't Worry about Patents 79

    Productivity Tips for Entrepreneurs 80

20 Book Recommendations from Elon Musk 82

FREE book 86

Your Reviews 87

A Note on Sources 88

Introduction

Elon Musk is known as one of the world's most outstanding entrepreneurs of our time. As the visionary engineer and inventor, he was behind the extraordinary success of PayPal, SpaceX, Tesla Inc. and Solar City that brought ground-breaking change to the world of finance, spacecraft technologies, car-making and energy industries.

Born and raised in South Africa, Musk moved to Canada in search of a better life, and now resides and works in the USA. He had a troubled childhood, was bullied at school, faced a hard time after the move to a new country and struggled financially. Today, he is one of the Top 100 wealthiest and most powerful men on the planet and is worth over 16 billion US dollars.

Virtually, he has become a citizen of the world who perceives his main mission in changing people's life for the better. Space exploration and making men space-faring civilizations are his major endeavors. He believes that in the near future, we will see humans as a multi-planetary species establishing human colonies on Mars.

Some think that he is an oddball; others take him for a naive dreamer obsessed with the idea of mankind's rescue and moving people to Mars. Though Elon Musk's concepts may look unrealistic at first glance, some of them have already materialized. Remarkable Tesla electric cars have won over people around the world, his Falcon rockets are already reusable; and it's fair to say that very soon, most houses in the US are going to be powered by solar roofs.

Elon Musk still speaks in his haltering South-African accent, but his words resonate universally. His life inspires. Unarguably, he knows better. This book features the best quotations of this extraordinary eager man whose space exploration pursuits seem to know no boundaries.

Part 1: LIFE LESSONS

Meaning of Life

1. "Life can't just be about solving problems; otherwise, what's the point? There's gotta be things that people find inspiring and make life worth living."

—Elon Musk at the World Government Summit in Dubai, February 13, 2017

2. "Now is the time to take risk.... You probably don't have kids. But as you get older, your obligations increase. And once you have a family, you start taking risks not just for yourself but for your family as well. It gets much harder to do things that might not work out. So now is the time to do that. Before you have those obligations, I would encourage you to take risks now. Do something bold. You won't regret it."

—Elon Musk's USC Commencement Speech, 2014

3. "You should take the approach that you're always some degree wrong. Your goal is to be less wrong."

— Elon Musk at the World Government Summit in Dubai, February 13, 2017

4. "We need to figure out how to have the things we love and not destroy the world."

— Forbes Life, March, 2012

5. "When I was a kid, I was wondering – what's the meaning of life, why are we here, what's it all about? I came to the conclusion that what really matters is trying to understand the right questions to ask. And the more that we can increase the scope and scale of human consciousness, the better we are able to ask these questions."

—Elon Musk at the World Government Summit in Dubai, February 13, 2017

6. "Life is too short for long-term grudges."

—Inc., July 21, 2016

7. "We are already a cyborg. You have a digital version of yourself, a partial version of yourself online in the form of your emails, your social media, and all the things that you do. We already have 'superpowers.'

You have more power than the president of the United States had 20 years ago. You can answer any question, you can video conference with anyone, anywhere. You can send messages to millions of people instantly. Just do incredible things."

—The Verge, June 2, 2016

8. "When I was in college, I wanted to be involved in things that would change the world. Now I am."

—Inc., July 21, 2016

9. "Now the output of goods and services will be extremely high. So with automation, there will come abundance. Almost everything will get very cheap. We'll all just end up doing universal basic income, it's going to be necessary.

The harder challenge is how do people then have meaning. A lot of people drive their meaning from their employment. So if you're not needed, if there's not a need for your labor, what's the meaning? Do you have meaning? Do you feel useless? That's a much harder problem to deal with."

—Elon Musk at the World Government Summit in Dubai, February 13, 2017

Childhood & Upbringing

10. "I didn't really have a primary nanny or anything. I just had a housekeeper who was there to make sure I didn't break anything. She wasn't watching me. I was off making explosives and reading books and building rockets and doing things that could have gotten me killed. I'm shocked that I have all my fingers. I was raised by books. Books, and then my parents."

—*Rolling Stone, November 15, 2017*

11. "I had a terrible upbringing. I had a lot of adversity growing up. One thing I worry about with my kids is they don't face enough adversity."

—*Business Insider, September 16, 2011*

12. "My mother somewhat overstates her role in raising me."

—*The New Yorker, August 24, 2009*

13. (Elon Musk on his parents' divorce): "I felt sorry for my father because my mother had all three kids. He seemed very sad and lonely by himself. So I thought, 'I can be company.' But I didn't really understand at the time what kind of person he was. It was not a good idea. He was such a terrible human being… My dad will have a carefully thought-out plan of evil. He will plan evil…. My dad was not physically violent with me. He was only physically violent when I was very young….

You have no idea about how bad. Almost every crime you can possibly think of, he has done. Almost every evil thing you could possibly think of, he has done. It's so terrible, you can't believe it."

—Rolling Stone, November 15, 2017

14. "I would just question things.... It would infuriate my parents that I wouldn't just believe them when they said something, because I'd ask them why. And then I'd consider whether that response made sense given everything else I knew."

—Inc., July 21, 2016

15. "When I was a little kid, I was really scared of the dark. But then I came to understand, dark just means the absence of photons in the visible wavelength – 400 to 700 nanometers.

Then I thought, 'It's really silly to be afraid of a lack of photons.' Then I wasn't afraid of the dark anymore after that."

—Bloomberg, June 10, 2014

16. "I wasn't born in America – I got here as fast as I could."

—PBS: Think Tank, December, 2007

17. "I don't have an issue with serving in the military per se, but serving in the South African army suppressing black people just didn't seem like a really good way to spend time."

—PBS: Wired Science, January, 2007

18. "Early in life, I did lots of risky things when I didn't have that much that was depending on me. Now, I have to be more cautious about risky things."

—Elon Musk's interview at SpaceX, TheHenryFord, June 26, 2008

Education

19. "I hated going to school when I was a kid. It was torture."

—Elon Musk's interview, Philosophy Workout, April, 2015

20. "I read all the comics I could buy, or that they let me read at the bookstores before chasing me away. I read everything I could get my hands on from when I woke up to when I went to sleep. At one point, I really ran out of books, so I started reading encyclopedia."

—Bloomberg, August 3, 2011

21. "[My father] was irrelevant. He paid nothing for college. My brother and I paid for college through scholarships, loans, and working two jobs simultaneously. The funding we raised for our first company came from a small group of random angel investors in Silicon Valley."

—Rolling Stone, November 15, 2017

22. "When I went to college, I rarely went to class. I'd just read the textbook and show up for exams."

—Bloomberg, August 3, 2011

23. "I didn't actually read many general business books, but I like reading biographies and autobiographies. Those are pretty helpful. For example, Franklin's. I would say he's one of the people I always admire. Franklin is pretty awesome.... He was an entrepreneur. He started from nothing. He was just a runaway kid."

—*Elon Musk's interview with Kevin Rose, YouTube, September, 2012*

24. "A business degree teaches you a lot of the terminologies. It introduces you to concepts that you would otherwise have to learn empirically. I think you can learn whatever you need to do to start a successful business either in school or out of school.

A school, in theory, should help accelerate that process, and oftentimes it does. It can be an efficient learning process; perhaps, more efficient than empirically learning lessons. There are examples of successful entrepreneurs who never graduated high school, and there are those that have PhDs. The important principle is to be dedicated to learning what you need to know, whether that is in school or empirically."

—*Stanford eCorner, 2003*

25. "I wouldn't recommend an MBA. I'd say no MBA needed. An MBA is a bad idea. It teaches people all sorts of wrong things.

They don't teach people to think in MBA schools. And the top MBA schools are the worst. Because they actually teach people that you must be special, and it causes people to close down their feedback loop and not rigorously examine when they are wrong."

—*APS News, November, 2013*

26. "In the United States especially, there's an over-allocation of talent in finance and law. Basically, too many smart people go into finance and law. This is both a compliment and a criticism. We should have fewer people doing law and fewer people doing finance and more people making stuff."

—*The Joe Rogan Experience, REV, May 7, 2020*

27. "Edison was a good role model; probably one of the biggest role models."

—*Elon Musk's interview at SpaceX, TheHenryFord.org, June 26, 2008*

Money & Debts

28. "Most people, when they make a lot of money, don't want to risk it. For me, it was never about money, but solving problems for the future of humanity."

—Smithsonian Magazine, December, 2012

29. "In America, it's pretty easy to keep yourself alive. So my threshold for existing was pretty low.

I figured I could be in some cheap apartment with my computer and be okay, and not starve....

So I was like, 'Oh, if I can live for a dollar a day – at least from a food cost standpoint – it's pretty easy to earn $30 in a month, so I'll probably be okay.'"

—The Washington Post, March 24, 2015

30. "I didn't have any money. In fact, I had negative money; I had huge student debts. I couldn't afford a place to stay and an office, so I just rented an office instead. I just slept on a futon and showered at YMCA (Young Man's Christian Association).

That's the best shape I've ever been – shower, workout, and you are good to go. There was an ISP on the floor below us; just a little tiny ISP. We drilled a hole through the floor and connected to their cable.

That gave us Internet connectivity for $100/month. We had an absurdly tiny burn rate. We also had a tiny revenue stream."

—*Stanford eCorner, October 8, 2003*

31. "Going from PayPal, I thought: 'Well, what are some of the other problems that are likely to most affect the future of humanity?' Not from the perspective, 'What's the best way to make money?'"

—*Business Insider, September 12, 2013*

32. "My proceeds from PayPal after tax were about $180 million. $100 million of that went into SpaceX, $70 into Tesla, and $10 into SolarCity. I literally had to borrow money for rent."

—*Startups.co, November 28, 2016*

33. "People would say, 'Did you hear the joke about the guy who made a small fortune in the space industry? Obviously, he started with a large one.' And so I tell people, 'I was trying to figure out the fastest way to turn a large fortune into a small one.' And they'd look at me, 'Is he serious?'…

It was a close call. Things almost didn't work out. We came very close to failure, but we managed to get through that point in 2008."

—*TED Talks, February, 2013*

34. "I had to take all of my reserve capital and invest it into Tesla. Which was very scary because it would obviously be quite sad to have the fruits of my labour with Zip2 and PayPal not amount to anything. But there was no question that I would do that, because Tesla was too important to let die."

—Financial Review, April 15, 2016

35. "Relative to others with a similar net worth, I don't spend much money on personal matters. I own no homes (not even my residence at this point), yachts or expensive artwork. My clothes are mostly jeans and t-shirts and I almost never take vacations, apart from kid related travel."

—Business Insider, July 8, 2010

Personal Life

36. "It's not as much fun being me as you think."

> —*Elon Musk at the World Government Summit in Dubai, February 13, 2017*

37. "My alcohol tolerance is not very high. But I tend to be a fuzzy bear when I drink. I go happy fuzzy."

> —*Rolling Stone, November 15, 2017*

38. "I would like to allocate more time to dating, though. I need to find a girlfriend. That's why I need to carve out just a little more time. I think maybe even another five to ten — how much time does a woman want a week? Maybe 10 hours? That's kind of the minimum? I don't know."

> —*Ashlee Vance, Elon Musk: Tesla, SpaceX and the Quest for a Fantastic Future, 2015*

39. "I will never be happy without having someone. Going to sleep alone kills me... It's not like I don't know what that feels like: being in a big empty house, and the footsteps echoing through the hallway, no one there – and no one on the pillow next to you. How do you make yourself happy in a situation like that?"

> —*Rolling Stone, November 15, 2017*

40. "As you get older, you tend to put on weight. Certainly, that's happening with me. The older I get like, 'Damn, sure harder to stay lean.' That's for sure. Speaking for myself, I'd rather eat tasty food and live a shorter life. Tasty food is great, it's one of the best things about life."

—The Joe Rogan Experience, REV, May 7, 2020

Engineering & Design

41. "Often comes as a surprise when people learn that 80% of my time is on engineering/design and just 20% on other stuff."

—*Elon Musk, Twitter, July 25, 2017*

42. "I'm a head engineer and chief designer as well as CEO, so I don't have to cave to some money guy. I encounter CEOs who don't know the details of their technology and that's ridiculous to me."

—*Smithsonian Magazine, December, 2012*

43. "A company is a group organized to create a product or service, and it is only as good as its people and how excited they are about creating. I do want to recognize a ton of super-talented people. I just happen to be the face of the companies."

—*Inc., July 21, 2016*

44. "It's unlikely that I'll do an Internet company again, not that I find the Internet boring. I'm relatively net savvy and interested in the Internet and what's going on. I don't ever want to be the grandpa who doesn't do email or something like that.

I'm trying to allocate my efforts to that which would most affect the future of humanity in a positive way. There's lots of entrepreneurial energy and financing headed towards the Internet, whereas, in certain sectors like automotive, solar, and space, you don't see new entrants. There's not a lot of capital going to startups and not a lot of entrepreneurs going to those arenas."

—Startups.co, November 28, 2016

45. "If you're going to make a product, make it beautiful. Even if it doesn't affect sales, I want it to be beautiful."

—Rolling Stone, November 15, 2017

Politics & Democracy

46. "We should try to make things happen for the right reason. We shouldn't give in to the politics. If we give in to that, we'll get the political system we deserve."

—All Things Digital, May 29, 2013

47. "Most likely, the form of government of Mars would be a direct democracy, not representative.... So it would be people voting directly on issues. And that's probably better because the potential for democracy is substantially diminished."

—Business Insider, October 25, 2016

48. "I've used the meetings I've had thus far to argue in favor of immigration and in favor of climate change. If I hadn't done that....

That wasn't on the agenda before, so maybe nothing will happen, but at least the words were said." – Elon Musk on meeting with Donald Trump.

—TED Talks, April, 2017

49. "The United States is more open to new ideas than any country in the world. And it becomes somewhat of a self-fulfilling prophecy in that because the United States is open to new ideas, it attracted people from around the world who had new ideas.

So now it's filled with people who like new ideas. And who aren't bound by history."

—Elon Musk's interview at SpaceX,
TheHenryFord.org, June 26, 2008

Mentality of a Samurai

50. "My mentality is that of a samurai. I would rather commit seppuku than fail."

>—Ashlee Vance, Elon Musk: Tesla, SpaceX and the Quest for a Fantastic Future, 2015

51. "I will never give up, and I mean never." – Elon Musk said in a defiant message to his employees after Falcon 1 loss.

>—Universe Today, December 24, 2015

52. "I am probably a bit crazy, but maybe that's a healthy sign. At the point at which you conclude, you're not crazy at all, then you probably are."

>—Startups.co, November 28, 2016

53. "I say something, and then it usually happens. Maybe not on schedule, but it usually happens."

>—The Independent, June Saturday 7, 2014

54. "Some people don't like change, but you need to embrace change if the alternative is disaster."

>—Daily Beast, April 25, 2011

55. "The first step is to establish that something is possible; then probability will occur."

>—Esquire, November 14, 2012

56. "No, I don't ever give up. I'd have to be dead or completely incapacitated."

—Stanford eCorner, October 8, 2003

Part 2: INCREDIBLE PROJECTS

Tesla

57. "I intend to stay with Tesla as far into the future as I can imagine, and there are a lot of exciting things that we have coming."

—TED Talks, April, 2017

58. "I love the thought of a car drifting apparently endlessly through space and perhaps being discovered by an alien race millions of years in the future." – Elon Musk loaded the Falcon Heavy with his own cherry-red Tesla Roadster carrying a spacesuit-clad mannequin named "Starman" in the driver's seat.

—Elon Musk, Twitter, December 2, 2017

59. "Sustainable energy will happen, no matter what. If there was no Tesla, if Tesla never existed, it would have to happen out of necessity. It's tautological. If you don't have sustainable energy, it means you have unsustainable energy. Eventually, you will run out, and the laws of economics will drive civilization towards sustainable energy, inevitably. The fundamental value of a company like Tesla is the degree to which it accelerates the advent of sustainable energy, faster than it would otherwise occur."

—TED Talks, April, 2017

60. "Even if there's a zombie apocalypse, you'll still be able to travel using the Tesla Supercharging system."

— *Autoblog, May 30, 2013*

61. "My goal was never to be the CEO of Tesla from the beginning. I had an interest in electric cars that goes back 20 years to when I was in college. In fact, I used to talk to my dates about electric cars. Probably not the best strategy. Since I was doing SpaceX, I knew that if I did try to start an electric car company and run it, that it would be extremely painful to run two companies. I really tried my hardest not to be the CEO of Tesla.

At any point, from day one, I could have been the CEO because I had majority control of the company, but I really tried not to. At the end of 2008, I had to commit all of my reserve capital to Tesla, that wasn't allocated to SpaceX. I felt I had to steer the ship directly. It was really not fun, super not fun."

—*Startups.co, November 28, 2016*

62. "The strategy of Tesla from the beginning has always been to start with a low volume, high priced car, then go to a medium volume, mid-priced car, and then low-priced, high volume."

—*Tonight on Charlie Rose, August 11, 2009*

63. "At the beginning, I hired a CEO to run Tesla, but it became apparent that he simply couldn't get the job done. Taking over was the only option I had. Now I have a great team, and most of my time is spent in engineering and design. That's my forte."

—GQ Magazine, 2013

64. "Almost every automaker has some electric vehicle program. They vary in seriousness. Some are very serious about transitioning entirely in electric and some are just dabbling in it. And some amazingly are still pursuing fuel cells, but I don't think that will last much longer. Something funny happened. Apparently, in order to motivate BMW executives, they showed a picture of me."

—TED Talks, April, 2017

65. "I thought the big car companies would be coming out with electric cars sooner."

—GQ Magazine, November 26, 2014

66. "We poured our heart into the car. Hope you love it."

—Elon Musk, Twitter, August 02, 2017

67. "When I spoke with someone about the Tesla Model S, I didn't really want to know what's right about the car. I want to know what's wrong about the car."

—HubSpot, October 05, 2017

68. "I've been in severe emotional pain for the last few weeks.... Severe. It took every ounce of will to be able to do the Model 3 event and not look like the most depressed guy around. For most of that day, I was morbid. And then I had to psych myself up: drink a couple of Red Bulls, hang out with positive people and then tell myself: 'I have all these people depending on me. All right, do it.'"

—Rolling Stone, November 15, 2017

SpaceX

69. "SpaceX is like Special Forces... we do the missions that others think are impossible. We have goals that are absurdly ambitious by any reasonable standard, but we're going to make them happen. We have the potential here at SpaceX to have an incredible effect on the future of humanity and life itself."

—SpaceX careers page, SpaceX.com

70. "I'd soon come to a conclusion that if something didn't happen to improve rocket technology, we'd be stuck on Earth forever. And the big aerospace companies had just had no interest in radical innovation.

All they wanted to do was try to make their old technology slightly better every year. And in fact, sometimes it would actually get worse. Particularly in rockets, it was pretty bad."

—Elon Musk's interview with Sam Altman,
Y Combinator, September, 2016

71. "The goal of SpaceX is to develop the technologies necessary to make life multi-planetary and establish self-sustaining settlements on Mars. And ultimately make life truly multi-planetary and that's one of the most important things that we could possibly do.

Because that will more than anything ensure the continuance of life as we know it and ensure that the light of consciousness on earth is not extinguished."

—Engineering.com, 2012

72. "SpaceX has the most advanced rockets in the world, but so far the advances have been evolutionary because the rockets are expendable — they end up in the ocean. The revolutionary breakthrough will come with rockets that are fully and rapidly reusable. We will never conquer Mars unless we do that. It'll be too expensive. The American colonies would never have been pioneered if the ships that crossed the ocean hadn't been reusable."

—Esquire, November 14, 2012

73. "I try to make it a really fun place to work, really enjoyable. I talk about the grand, the vision of SpaceX, where we wanna go, what we wanna do – we wanna take people to orbit and beyond.

We ultimately want to be the company that makes a difference in extension of life beyond Earth – which is one of the most important things that life itself could achieve.

And so, you construct this great Holy Grail potential in the future. You have to stay grounded in the short term, because if you don't do things that pay the bills, you're not gonna achieve the ultimate launch and objective.

But it's nice to have that sort of Holy Grail – long-term potential out there as inspiration for coming to work."

—Elon Musk's interview at SpaceX, TheHenryFord.org, June 26, 2008

Solar Power

74. "Eventually, almost all houses will have a solar roof. The thing is to consider the time scale here to be probably on the order of 40 or 50 years. So on average, a roof is replaced every 20 to 25 years.

But you don't start replacing all roofs immediately. But eventually, 15 years from now, it will be unusual to have a roof that does not have solar."

—TED Talks, April, 2017

75. "It's a fair statement to say that most houses in the US have enough roof area to power all the needs of the house."

—TED Talks, April, 2017

76. "I'm confident solar will be the single largest source of energy for humanity in the future."

—Elon Musk's interview at Oxford, Oxford Martin School, 2012

77. "We've got this giant fusion generator in the sky called the sun, and we just need to tap a little bit of that energy for purposes of human civilization.

What most people know but don't realize they know is that the world is almost entirely solar-powered already. If the sun wasn't there, we'd be a frozen ice ball at three degrees Kelvin, and the sun powers the entire system of precipitation. The whole ecosystem is solar-powered."

—TED Talks, February, 2013

78. "Solar will beat everything, hands down, including natural gas.... It must, actually. If it doesn't, we're in deep trouble."

—TED Talks, February, 2013

Autonomous Cars

79. "My guess is in probably ten years, it will be very unusual for cars to be built that are not fully autonomous…. So getting in a car will be like getting in an elevator. You just tell it where you want to go and it takes you there with extreme levels of safety. And that will be normal. For elevators there used to be elevator operators, you get in and the big guy is moving a lever. Now you just get in and you press the button and that's taken for granted. So autonomy will be widespread."

—Elon Musk at the World Government Summit in Dubai, February 13, 2017

80. "One thing that has been quite disturbing to me is the degree of media coverage of Autopilot crashes…. [It] is basically almost none relative to the paucity of media coverage of the 1.2 million people that die every year in manual crashes…. And think carefully about this because if in writing some article that's negative you effectively dissuade people from using autonomous vehicles, you're killing people."

—Business Insider, October 25, 2016

81. "Absolutely this is what will happen: there will be a shared autonomy fleet where you buy your car, and you can choose to use that car exclusively, you could choose to have it be used only by friends and family, only by other drivers who are rated five stars, you can choose to share it some times but not other times. That's 100 percent what will occur, it's just a question of when."

—*TED Talks, April, 2017*

82. "In the distant future, people may outlaw driving cars because it's too dangerous. You can't have a person driving a two-ton death machine."

—*Elon Musk's interview, GPU Technology Conference, 2015*

83. "There's some chance that any time a human driver gets in a car, that they will have an accident that is their fault. It's never zero. So really the key threshold for autonomy is how much better does autonomy need to be than a person before you can rely on it?"

—*TED Talks, April, 2017*

84. "A lot of people think that when you make cars autonomous, they'll be able to go faster and that will alleviate congestion. And to some degree that will be true, but once you have shared autonomy, where it's much cheaper to go by car and you got point to point, the affordability of going in a car will be better than that of a bus. It will cost less than a bus ticket, so the amount of driving that will occur will be much great with shared autonomy and actually traffic will get far worse."

—TED Talks, April, 2017

85. "It's going to be a great convenience to have an autonomous car, but there are many people who their jobs it is to drive. In fact, it might be the single largest employer of people is driving in various forms. Then we need to figure out new roles for what do those people do, but it will be very disruptive and very quick."

—Elon Musk at the World Government Summit in Dubai, February 13, 2017

Journey to Mars

86. "Mars colonization is something I hope to be a part of."

—Elon Musk, Instagram, August 04, 2017

87. "I would like to die on Mars, just not on impact."

—Elon Musk at the SXSW Conference, March 9, 2013

88. "I do wanna go to space – and eventually it would be really cool if I could go to Mars. That would be super awesome. But this is not about me getting to space; it's really about enabling others to get to space. It's about enabling the extension of life beyond Earth. So I'd like to go in the first one. If I didn't have so much depending on me, I would, actually."

—Elon Musk's interview at SpaceX, TheHenryFord.org, June 26, 2008

89. "The lessons of history would suggest that civilisations move in cycles. You can track that back quite far – the Babylonians, the Sumerians, followed by the Egyptians, the Romans, China. We're obviously in a very upward cycle right now, and hopefully, that remains the case. But it may not.

There could be some series of events that cause that technology level to decline. Given that this is the first time in 4.5bn years where it's been possible for humanity to extend life beyond Earth, it seems like we'd be wise to act while the window was open and not count on the fact it will be open a long time."

—The Guardian, July 17, 2013

90. (The odds of the Mars colony): "Oddly enough, I actually think they're pretty good. I'm certain that success is one of the possible outcomes for establishing a self-sustaining Mars colony, a growing Mars colony. I'm certain that is possible. Whereas until maybe a few years ago, I was not sure that success was even one of the possible outcomes.

In terms of having some meaningful number of people going to Mars, this is potentially something that can be accomplished in about ten years. Maybe sooner; maybe nine years. I need to make sure that SpaceX doesn't die between now and then and that I don't die. Or if I do die, that someone takes over who will continue that."

—Elon Musk's interview with Sam Altman,
Y Combinator, September, 2016

91. "If you're going to choose a place to die, then Mars is probably not a bad choice."

—Business Insider, October 25, 2016

92. "People focus on the problems here on Earth, but some small amount of money – less than one percent of our resources — should be spent on establishing colonies on Mars and making humanity a multi-planet species.

It's a matter of priorities. It is less important than health care, for example, but more important than cosmetics. I'm in favor of cosmetics. I like them, they are great but, you know...a lipstick or a colony on Mars?"

—One-on-one with Elon Musk, MIT Centennial Symposium, October 24, 2014

93. "The first journey to Mars is going to be really very dangerous.... The risk of fatality will be high. There's just no way around it."

—Business Insider, October 25, 2016

94. "I hope we are out there on Mars and maybe beyond Mars, the moons of Jupiter. I hope we are traveling frequently throughout the solar system perhaps preparing for missions to nearby star systems. All of this is possible within fifty years. And that will be very excited to do that."

—Elon Musk at the World Government Summit in Dubai, February 13, 2017

95. "I still believe this: If we continue upon the Apollo program and get to Mars and beyond, that will seem far more important in historical context than anything else we do today. The day multi-planetary species come about, things like the Soviet Union will be forgotten or merely remembered by arcane historical scholars. Things like the invasion of Iraq won't even be a footnote."

—Pennsylvania Gazette, November 4, 2008

96. "Space races are exciting."

—Reuters, February 6, 2018

97. "It would take six months to get to Mars if you go there slowly, with optimal energy cost.... Then it would take eighteen months for the planets to realign. Then it would take six months to get back, though I can see getting the travel time down to three months pretty quickly. It is entirely manageable if America has the will."

—Esquire, November 14, 2012

98. "SpaceX, or some combination of companies and governments, needs to make progress in the direction of making life multi-planetary, of establishing a base on another planet, on Mars – being the only realistic option – and then building that base up until we're a true multi-planet species."

—TED Talks, February, 2013

Exciting Future

99. "The value of beauty and inspiration is very much underrated, no question. But I want to be clear. I'm not trying to be anyone's savior. I'm just trying to think about the future and not be sad."

—TED Talks, April, 2017

100. "I did build rockets when I was a kid, but I didn't think I'd be involved in this. It was really more from the standpoint of what are the things that need to happen in order for the future to be an exciting and inspiring one?

And I really think there's a fundamental difference, if you look into the future, between a humanity that is a space-faring civilization, that's out there exploring the stars, on multiple planets, and that's really exciting, compared with one where we are forever confined to Earth until some eventual extinction event."

—TED Talks, February, 2013

101. "It's important to have a future that is inspiring and appealing. There have to be reasons that you get up in the morning and you want to live. Why do you want to live? What's the point? What inspires you? What do you love about the future?

And if we're not out there, if the future does not include being out there among the stars and being a multiplanet species, I find that it's incredibly depressing if that's not the future that we're going to have."

—TED Talks, April, 2017

102. "I'm interested in things that change the world or that affect the future, and wondrous, new technology where you see it, and you're like, 'Wow, how did that even happen? How is that possible?'"

—Inc., July 21, 2016

103. "If you get up in the morning and think the future is going to be better, it is a bright day. Otherwise, it's not."

—YourStory, August 20, 2019

Hyperloop

104. "We have planes, trains, automobiles and boats.... What if there was a fifth mode?"

—The Atlantic, July 21, 2012

105. "Short of figuring out real teleportation, which would, of course, be awesome (someone please do this), the only option for super-fast travel is to build a tube over or under the ground that contains a special environment."

—Business Insider, June 4, 2016

106. "The solution to urban congestion is a network of tunnels under cities. I don't mean a 2D plane of tunnels. I mean tunnels that go many levels deep.

So you can always go deeper than you can go up, like that the deepest mines are taller than the tallest buildings.

So you could have tunnels – a network of tunnels that has 20, 30, 40, 50 levels; as many levels as you want really, and so given that you can overcome the congestion situation in any city in the world.

The challenge is just figuring out how do you build tunnels quickly and at low cost and with high safety.

So if tunneling technology can be improved to the point where you can build tunnels, fast, cheap, and safe, then that would completely get rid of any traffic situations in cities."

> —*Elon Musk at the World Government Summit in Dubai, February 13, 2017*

107. "We've got a pet snail called Gary.... So, Gary is capable of going 14 times faster than a tunnel boring machine.... We want to beat Gary. He's not a patient little fellow. That will be victory. Victory is beating the snail."

> —*TED Talks, April, 2017*

Democratization of AI Technology

108. "One of the most troubling questions is artificial intelligence. And I don't mean narrow AI like vehicle autonomy I would put in the narrow AI class. It's narrowly trying to achieve a certain function. But deep artificial intelligence or what is sometimes called artificial general intelligence where you can have AI that is much smarter than the smartest human on Earth. This is a dangerous situation."

—Elon Musk at the World Government Summit in Dubai, February 13, 2017

109. "If you're not concerned about AI safety, you should be. Vastly more risk than North Korea.... 'In the end, the machines will win.'"

—Elon Musk, Twitter, August 12, 2017

110. "In terms of things that are most like to affect the future of humanity, AI is probably the single biggest item in the near-term that's likely to affect humanity. So, it's very important that we have the advent of AI in a good way.

If you could look into the crystal ball and to the future, you would like that outcome because it is something that could go wrong. We really need to make sure it goes right. That's the most important thing, right now, the most pressing item."

—Elon Musk's interview with Sam Altman, Y Combinator, September, 2016

111. "We need to be very careful with artificial intelligence.… I'm increasingly inclined to think that there should be some regulatory oversight, maybe at the national and international level, just to make sure that we don't do something very foolish. With artificial intelligence we're summoning the demon."

—Business Insider, October 25, 2016

112. "The best of the available alternatives that I can come up with, and maybe someone else can come up with a better approach or better outcome, is that we achieve democratization of AI technology. Meaning that no one company or small set of individuals has control over advanced AI technology. That's very dangerous.

It could also get stolen by somebody bad, some evil dictator or country could send their intelligence agency to go steal it and gain control. It just becomes a very unstable situation, if you've got any incredibly powerful AI. You just don't know who's going to control that. So it's not that I think that the risk is that the AI would develop a will of its own right off the bat. The concern is that someone may use it in a way that is bad."

*—Elon Musk's interview with Sam Altman,
Y Combinator, September, 2016*

113. "Today, if you don't bring your phone along it's like you have missing limb syndrome. It feels like something's really missing. We're already partly a cyborg or an AI symbiote, essentially it's just that the data rate to the electronics is slow. Especially output, like, you're just going with your thumbs. I mean what's your data rate? Optimistically, a hundred bits per second. That's being generous."

—The Joe Rogan Experience, REV, May 7, 2020

114. "I don't love the idea of being a house cat, but what's the solution? I think one of the solutions that seems maybe the best is to add an AI layer. A third digital layer that could work well and 'symbiotically' with the rest of your body."

—Business Insider, October 25, 2016

115. "The future is going to be weird. In the future, you will be able to save and replay memories. You could basically store your memories as a backup and restore the memories. You could potentially download them into a new body or into a robot body...

Over time we could give somebody super vision." – with a device surgically implanted into the skull of a pig named Gertrude, Elon Musk demonstrated his startup Neuralink's technology to build a digital link between brains and computers.

—CNET.com, August 29, 2020

116. "We may be able to implant a neural link in less than a year in a person. For version one of the device, it would be implanted in your skull. So you take out a chunk of skull and put the Neuralink device in there. You'd insert the electrode threads very carefully into the brain, and then you stitch it up, and you wouldn't even know that somebody has it.

It can interface anywhere in your brain. It could be something that helps cure eyesight, like returns your eyesight even if you've lost your optic nerve."

—The Joe Rogan Experience, REV, May 7, 2020

117. "I do worry that if robotics get too good, what's the point of us?"

—Elon Musk's interview at Oxford, Oxford Martin School, 2012

118. "Climate change is the biggest threat that humanity faces this century, except for AI. I keep telling people this. I hate to be Cassandra here, but it's all fun and games until somebody loses an eye."

—Rolling Stone, November 15, 2017

Simulated Reality

119. "There's a billion-to-one chance we're living in base reality."

—Business Insider, October 25, 2016

120. "Arguably we should hope that that's true, because otherwise if civilization stops advancing, that may be due to some calamitous event that erases civilization.... So maybe we should be hopeful that this is a simulation, because otherwise.... We are either going to create simulations indistinguishable from reality or civilization ceases to exist."

—Business Insider, October 25, 2016

121. "Now you can see a video game that's photo-realistic, almost photo-realistic, and millions of people playing simultaneously. And you see where things are going with virtual reality and augmented reality. And if you extrapolate that out into the future with any rate of progress at all even 0.1% or something like that a year, then eventually those games will be indistinguishable from reality. They will be so realistic you will not be able to tell the difference from that game and the reality as we know it. And then how do we know that that didn't happen in the past and that we're not in one of those games ourselves."

—Elon Musk at the World Government Summit in Dubai, February 13, 2017

122. "I've had so many simulation discussions it's crazy. In fact, it got to the point where basically every conversation was the AI-slash-simulation conversation, and my brother and I finally agreed that we'd ban any such conversations if we're ever in a hot tub. Because that really kills the magic." – Elon Musk on whether humans exist in another civilization's video game."

—Business Insider, June 4, 2016

123. "Who controls the memes, controls the Universe."

—Elon Musk, Twitter, June 26, 2020

Part 3: SUCCESS LESSONS

Why Failure is Fine

124. "I try to push people to do new and different things. There has to be a culture where failure is fine if you thought it through and accessed the risks."

—Elon Musk at the Chicago Economics Club Dinner, April 2012

125. "If something's important enough, you should try. Even if the probable outcome is failure."

—Inc., July 21, 2016

126. "When starting SpaceX, I thought the odds of success were less than 10% and I just accepted that actually probably I would just lose everything. But that maybe would make some progress. If we could just move the ball forward, even if we died, maybe some other company could pick up the baton and keep moving it forward, so we'd still do some good. Same with Tesla. I thought the odds of a car company succeeding were extremely low."

—Elon Musk's interview with Sam Altman, Y Combinator, September, 2016

127. "It's like the Nike slogan: 'Just Do It'. You know, 'Just showing up is half the battle.' You've got to try hard to do it, and don't be afraid of failure. But you also need to be rooted in reality.

You've gotta not be afraid to innovate, but also don't delude yourself into thinking something's working when it's not, or you're going to get fixated on a bad solution. And also, don't be afraid of new arenas: you can get a book, you can learn something, and experiment with your hands, and just make it happen. Find a way or make a way to make something happen."

—Elon Musk's interview at SpaceX, TheHenryFord.org, June 26, 2008

128. "There's a tremendous bias against taking risks. Everyone is trying to optimize their ass-covering."

—Inc., July 21, 2016

129. "It's OK to have your eggs in one basket as long as you control what happens to that basket."

—Inc., July 21, 2016

130. "Failure is an option here. If things are not failing, you are not innovating enough."

—Business Insider, September 12, 2013

131. "People are too afraid to try things. They shouldn't be afraid of failing. They should just go and do it."

—SoulPancake, March 18, 2013

132. "If there are two paths and we have to choose one thing or the other, and one wasn't obviously better than the other, then rather than spend a lot of time trying to figure out which one is slightly better, we'll just pick one and do it. Sometimes we'd be wrong and we picked the suboptimal path. Often, it's better to pick a path and do it than to just vacillate on a choice."

—Stanford eCorner, October 8, 2003

How to Deal with Fear

133. "I feel fear quite strongly, so it's not like I don't have fear. If it's important enough, then I just override the fear. Ignore it. But it does cause me a lot of stress and anguish."

>*—Christopher Kai interviews Elon Musk, March, 2014*

134. "I wouldn't say I have a lack of fear. In fact, I'd like my fear emotion to be less because it's very distracting and fries my nervous system."

>*—Inc., July 21, 2016*

135. "There are just times when something is important enough that you believe in it that you do it in spite of fear. People shouldn't think, 'I feel fear about this and therefore I shouldn't do it.' It's normal to feel fear. You'd have to have something mentally wrong with you if you don't feel fear. Actually, something that can be helpful is fatalism, to some degree. If you just accept the probabilities, then that diminishes fear."

>*—Elon Musk's interview with Sam Altman, Y Combinator, September, 2016*

136. "It is possible for ordinary people to choose to be extraordinary."

>*—Inc., July 21, 2016*

Listen to Negative Feedback

137. "It's very important to have a feedback loop, where you're constantly thinking about what you've done and how you could be doing it better. That's the single best piece of advice: constantly think about how you could be doing things better and questioning yourself."

—*Inc., July 21, 2016*

138. "You want to be extra rigorous about making the best possible thing you can. Find everything that's wrong with it and fix it."

—*Business Insider, September 12, 2013*

139. "Always seek negative feedback, even though it can be mentally painful.... I find the single biggest error people make is to ignore constructive, negative feedback."

—*Investor's Business Daily, August 21, 2012*

140. "Seek critical feedback, ask [friends] what's wrong. You often have to draw it out in a nuanced way because friends don't want to tell you exactly what's wrong because they don't want to hurt your feelings, but they often know.

So that can be really helpful. And then you keep trying to make it better and better. And then if your product/service is sufficiently better than whatever else is out there, or if there's nothing else like it, then your company will succeed."

—Hangout with Elon Musk and Sir Richard Branson, Google for Startups, August 8, 2013

How to Get New Ideas

141. "It's something of a cliché, but a lot of my ideas nowadays come to me when I'm in the shower... It's because I've been thinking about them, the mind processing them subconsciously while I'm sleeping, and what's the first thing you do when you get up in the morning? You take a shower."

—Queen's Alumni Review, Issue #1, 2013

142. There are times, late at night, when I pace. If I'm trying to solve a problem, and I think I've got some elements of it kind of close to being figured out, I'll pace for hours trying to think it through."

—Queen's Alumni Review, Issue #1, 2013

Innovative Thinking

143. "What makes innovative thinking happen? I think it's really a mindset. You have to decide."

—Inc., July 21, 2016

144. "When Henry Ford made cheap, reliable cars, people said, 'Nah, what's wrong with a horse?' That was a huge bet he made, and it worked."

—Inc., July 21, 2016

145. "When somebody has a breakthrough innovation, it is rarely one little thing. Very rarely, it is one little thing. It's usually a whole bunch of things that collectively amount to a huge innovation."

—Elon Musk's interview at SpaceX, TheHenryFord.org, June 26, 2008

146. "People are mistaken when they think that technology just automatically improves. It does not automatically improve. It only improves if a lot of people work very hard to make it better, and actually it will by itself degrade.

You look at great civilizations like Ancient Egypt, and they were able to make the pyramids, and they forgot how to do that. And then the Romans, they built these incredible aqueducts. They forgot how to do it."

—TED Talks, April, 2017

Persistence & Patience

147. "Patience is a virtue, and I'm learning patience. It's a tough lesson."

—Wired, August 5, 2008

148. "Persistence is very important. You should not give up unless you are forced to give up. You have to be cautious in always saying one should always persist and never give up because there actually are times when you should give up because you're doing something in error. But if you're convinced that what you're doing is correct then you should never give up."

—Inc., March 8, 2016

149 "When something is important enough, you do it even if the odds are not in your favor."

—Elon Musk at The Late Show with Stephen Colbert, 2015

Work Like Crazy

150. "I work a lot. I mean, a lot."

—TED Talks, February, 2013

151. "I'm available 24/7 to help solve issues, call me at 3 a.m on a Sunday morning. I don't care."

—Bloomberg, August 3, 2011

152. "Work like hell. You just have to put in 80- to 100-hour weeks every week. [This] improves the odds of success. If other people are putting in 40-hour workweeks and you're putting in 100-hour workweeks, then even if you're doing the same thing, you know that you will achieve in four months what it takes them a year to achieve."

—Inc., July 21, 2016

153. "The first time I took a week off, the Orbital Sciences rocket exploded, and Richard Branson's rocket exploded. In that same week, the second time I took a week off, my rocket exploded. The lesson here is don't take a week off."

—Elon Musk interviewed on Danish TV, September 27, 2015

154. "I can sort of figure out what's the right amount of sleep. I found I can drop below a certain threshold of sleep. Although I would be awake more hours, and I can sustain it, I would get less done because mental accuracy would be affected. I found generally the right amount for me is 6-6.5 hrs."

—*CHM Revolutionaries: An Evening with Elon Musk*, 2013

155. "Meetings are what happens when people aren't working."

—*GQ Magazine*, December 31, 2008

156. "If you're joining Tesla, you're joining a company to work hard. We're not trying to sell you a bill of goods. If you can go work for another company and then maybe you can work a 40-hour workweek. But if you work for Tesla, the minimum is really a 50-hour week and there are times when it'll be 60- to 80-hour weeks.

If somebody is hourly, they receive time-and-a-half, but if somebody is salary, then we do cash and stock bonuses for going above and beyond the call of duty.

So we try to make it fair compensation, but the general understanding is that if you're at Tesla, you're choosing to be at the equivalent of Special Forces. There's the regular Army, and that's fine, but if you are working at Tesla, you're choosing to step up your game. And that has pluses and minuses. It's cool to be Special Forces, but it also means you're working your ass off. It's not for everyone."

—Elon Musk's interview with Autoblog,
September 7, 2012

The Biggest Mistake

157. "One of the biggest mistakes people generally make, and I'm guilty of it too, is wishful thinking. You want something to be true even if it isn't true; and so you ignore... the real truth because of what you want to be true. This is a very difficult trap to avoid, and I find myself in having problems with."

—Elon Musk at the World Government Summit in Dubai, February 13, 2017

158. "The biggest mistake in general that I've made and I'm trying to correct for that is to put too much weighting on somebody's talent and not enough on personality. I've made that mistake several times. In fact, I'd say 'I'm not going to make that mistake again' and then I would make it again. It actually matters whether somebody has a good heart."

—Elon Musk at the SXSW Conference, March 9, 2013

159. "Don't work yourself to death to cover your mistakes.... I was very naive and much stupider than I am now. I wish I could go back and give myself a slap on my face.... I was working crazy hours. I would literally sleep under my desk to avoid going home because that'd just take time... I was trying to make up for my mistakes by working really, really hard. Instead, acknowledge your mistakes, fix them if you can, and move on if you can't."

—Business Insider, September 16, 2011

Make Something Valuable to People

160. "If somebody is doing something useful to the rest of society, that's a good thing. It doesn't have to change the world if you make something that has high value to people....

And frankly, even if it's just a little game or some improvement in photo sharing or something, if it has a small amount of good for a large number of people, I think that's fine. Stuff doesn't need to change the world just to be good."

—Elon Musk's interview with Sam Altman,
Y Combinator, September, 2016

161. "You can get a doctorate on many things that ultimately do not a have practical bearing on the world. And I really was just trying to be useful. That's the optimization. It's like, 'What can I do that would actually be useful?'"

—Elon Musk's interview with Sam Altman,
Y Combinator, September, 2016

Train Yourself to Think Differently

162. "Generally, [other people's] thinking process is too bound by convention or analogy to prior experiences. So it's very rare that people try to think of something on a first principles basis. They'll say, 'We'll do that because it's always been done that way.' Or they'll not do it because, 'Nobody has ever done that. So it must not be good.'

But that's just a ridiculous way to think. You have to build up the reasoning from the ground up from first principles as in the phrase that's used in physics. So you look at the fundamentals and construct your reasoning from that and then see if you have a conclusion that works or doesn't work. And it may or may not be different from what people have done in the past. It's harder to think that way."

—Elon Musk's interview at SpaceX, TheHenryFord.org, June 26, 2008

163. "I'd recommend studying the thinking process around physics, not the equations. The equations certainly helpful, but the way of thinking in physics is the best framework for understanding things that are counterintuitive."

—Elon Musk at the World Government Summit in Dubai, February 13, 2017

164. "Most of our life, we get through life by reasoning by analogy, which essentially means copying what other people do with slight variations. And you have not to do that."

—TED Talks, February, 2013

Tell the Truth

165. "Lots of people say that no matter if you are right or wrong, you don't battle with the New York Times. To hell with that, I would rather tell the truth and suffer the consequences even if they are negative."

—Bloomberg, February, 2013

166. "Being precise about the truth works. Truthful and precise. I try to tell people, 'You don't have to read between the lines with me. I'm saying the lines!'"

—Rolling Stone, November 15, 2017

Part 4: BRILLIANT ADVICE FOR ENTREPRENEURS

How to Create a Successful Company

167. "Great companies are built on great products."

—Inc., July 21, 2016

168. "A lot of companies get confused. They spend money on things that don't actually make the product better. So, for example at Tesla, we've never spent any money on advertising. We put all the money into R&D and manufacturing and design to try to make the car as good as possible. And I think that's the way to go, so for any given company, just keep thinking about, 'Are these efforts that people are expending, are they resulting in a better product or service?', and if they're not, stop those efforts."

—Elon Musk USC Commencement Speech, 2014

169. "I'd strongly recommend someone to just focus on one company and throw as many hours at it as you possibly can. Really work morning to night. Think about it in your sleep. Seven days a week. No breaks. That's what you should do when you are starting a company."

—Inc., August 08, 2013

170. "Starting a company is like staring into the abyss and eating glass. And there's some truth to that."

—Khan Academy, April 17, 2013

171. "If you're trying to create a company, it's like baking a cake. You have to have all the ingredients in the right proportion."

—Inc., July 21, 2016

172. "I don't create companies for the sake of creating companies, but to get things done."

—Inc., July 21, 2016

173. "People think creating a company is fun, it's really not that fun. There are periods of fun, and there are periods where they are just awful. Particularly, if you start a company, you actually have a distillation of all the worst problems of the company.

There's no point in spending your time on things that are going right, so you only spend your time on things that are going wrong. There will be things that are going wrong that other people can't take care of, you have a filter for the crappiest problem in the company.

You have to feel quite compelled to do it and have a fairly high pain threshold.

You've got to do the problems your company needs you to work on, not the problems you want to work on, and that goes on for a long time."

—Khan Academy, April 17, 2013

174. "Starting and growing a business is as much about the innovation, drive, and determination of the people behind it as the product they sell."

—Inc., July 21, 2016

175. "If you're creating a company or if you're joining a company, the most important thing is to attract great people. So, either join a group that's amazing, that you really respect, or if you're building a company, you've got to gather great people.

All a company is a group of people that are gathered together to create a product or service. And so, depending on how talented and hardworking that group is, and the degree to which they are focused cohesively and in a good direction, that will determine the success of the company. So, do everything you can to gather great people if you're creating a company."

—Elon Musk's USC Commencement Speech, 2014

176. "Don't delude yourself into thinking something's working when it's not, or you're gonna get fixated on a bad solution."

—Inc., July 21, 2016

177. "Talent is extremely important. It's like a sports team, the team that has the best individual player will often win, but then there's a multiplier from how those players work together and the strategy they employ."

—Inc., July 21, 2016

Advice on Raising Capital

178. "The best way to attract venture capital is to try and come up with a demonstration of whatever product or service it is and ideally take that as far as you can. Just see if you can sell that to real customers and start generating some momentum. The further along you can get with that, the more likely you are to get funding."

—*Inc., March 8, 2016*

Qualities of Prosperous Entrepreneurs

179. "Successful entrepreneurs probably come in all sizes, shapes and flavors. I'm not sure there's any one particular thing.... An obsessive nature with respect to the quality of the product is very important, so being obsessive and impulsive is a good thing in this context.

Really liking what you do, whatever area you get into, even if you are the best of the best, there always a chance of failure, so it's important that you really like what you are doing, If you don't like it, life is too short. If you like what you are doing, you'll think about it even when you are not working, it's something your mind is drawn to, you just really can't make it work."

—*Stanford eCorner, October 8, 2003*

180. "You shouldn't do things differently just because they're different. They need to be ... better."

—*Inc., July 21, 2016*

Hire Smart and Creative People

181. "People work better when they know what the goal is and why. It is important that people look forward to coming to work in the morning and enjoy working."

—Inc., July 21, 2016

182. "When you struggle with a problem, that's when you understand it.... When I interview someone to work at one of the companies [I ask them to] tell me the problems they've worked on and how they solved them. If someone was really the person that solved it, they'd be able to answer multiple levels. They'd be able to go down to the brass tacks. And if they weren't [then] they'll get stuck. Then you can say, 'Oh this person was not really the person who solved it because anyone who struggled hard with a problem never forgets it.'"

—Business Insider, December 26, 2013,

183. "As much as possible, avoid hiring M.B.A.'s. M.B.A. programs don't teach people how to create companies ... our position is that we hire someone in spite of an M.B.A., not because of one."

—Inc., September 19, 2014

184. "The problem is that at a lot of big companies, process becomes a substitute for thinking. You're encouraged to behave like a little gear in a complex

machine. Frankly, it allows you to keep people who aren't that smart, who aren't that creative."

—Inc., July 21, 2016

185. "Every person in your company is a vector. Your progress is determined by the sum of all vectors."

—HubSpot, October 2017

186. "It is a mistake to hire huge numbers of people to get a complicated job done. Numbers will never compensate for talent in getting the right answer (two people who don't know something are no better than one). [They] will tend to slow down progress and make the task incredibly expensive."

—Inc., July 21, 2016

What a Brand Is

187. "Brand is just a perception, and perception will match reality over time. Sometimes it will be ahead, other times it will be behind. But brand is simply a collective impression some have about a product."

—Inc., July 21, 2016

188. "The real way that brand happens is we make good products, and then people look at that product and say 'Ok', if a company can make that product, the other things that the company makes will also be good. And that's what a brand is, it's real simple."

—Tesla Motors, Inc. annual shareholder meeting, June 4, 2013

189. "I do think there is a lot of potential if you have a compelling product and people are willing to pay a premium for that. That is what Apple has shown. You can buy a much cheaper cell phone or laptop, but Apple's product is so much better than the alternative, and people are willing to pay that premium."

—Inc., July 21, 2016

Don't Worry about Patents

190. "We don't worry too much about intellectual property, paperwork and legal stuff, we are very focused on building the best product that we possibly could. Both Zip2 and PayPal were very product-focused companies. We were incredibly obsessed about how do we build something that would really be the best possible customer experience. That was a far more effective selling tool than having a giant sales force or taking up marketing gimmicks or 12-step processes or whatever."

—Stanford eCorner, October 8, 2003

191. "We don't patent. Since our primary competitors are national governments, the enforceability of patents is questionable."

—TED Talks, February, 2013

192. "Technology leadership is not defined by patents, which history has repeatedly shown to be small protection indeed against a determined competitor, but rather by the ability of a company to attract and motivate the world's most talented engineers. We believe that applying the open-source philosophy to our patents will strengthen rather than diminish Tesla's position in this regard."

—Tesla.com, 2014

Productivity Tips for Entrepreneurs

193. "The single best piece of advice: constantly think about how you could be doing things better and questioning yourself."

—Inc., July 21, 2016

194. "One thing important is to try not to serialize dependencies, put as many elements in parallel as possible as a lot of things have a gestation period, and it's very hard to accelerate that gestation period.

If you can have all those things gestating in parallel, then that is one way to substantially accelerate your timeline. People tend to serialize things too much."

—Stanford eCorner, October 8, 2003

195. "Better to do something good and be late than bad and be early."

—Rolling Stone, November 15, 2017

196. "There's a big leap between making that first prototype and actually manufacturing it in a large quantity."

—Elon Musk's interview at SpaceX, TheHenryFord.org, June 26, 2008

197. "The path to the CEO's office should not be through the CFO's office, and it should not be

through the marketing department. It needs to be through engineering and design."

—Inc., July 21, 2016

198. "Stay very focused on the quality of the product. People get really wrapped up in all sorts of esoteric notions of how to manage etc., [but] I think people should get much more focused on the product itself – how do you make the product incredibly compelling to a customer – just become maniacally focused on building it better."

— FUSE, June 29, 2011,

199. "It's very important to like the people you work with. Otherwise, life [and] your job is gonna be quite miserable."

—Inc., July 21, 2016

20 Book Recommendations from Elon Musk

1. **The Foundation trilogy by Isaac Asimov**

   "It's a futuristic version of Gibbon's Decline and Fall of the Roman Empire. Let's say you were at the peak of the Roman empire, what would you do, what action could you take to minimize decline?" — Elon Musk

2. **The Lord of the Rings by Tolkien, J. R. R.**

   "The heroes of the books I read … always felt a duty to save the world." — Elon Musk

3. **Benjamin Franklin: An American Life by Walter Isaacson**

   "I like Franklin's biography by Isaacson, it's really good.… It was interesting to see how he is creating his business, then go to science and politics. I could say he is one of the people I most admire. He did what needed to be done, at the time it needed to be done." — Elon Musk

4. **Einstein: His Life and Universe by Walter Isaacson**

5. **Tesla: Inventor of the Electrical Age by W. Bernard Carlson**

6. **Howard Hughes: His Life and Madness by Donald L. Barlett and James B. Steele**

"May be a cautionary tale, he is sort of an interesting fella." — Elon Musk

7. **Structures: Or Why Things Don't Fall Down by J.E. Gordon**

"There's a good book on structural design called 'Structures: Or Why Things Don't Fall Down.' It is really, really good if you want a primer on structural design." — Elon Musk

8. **Ignition!: An Informal History of Liquid Rocket Propellants by John D. Clark**

"There is a good book on rocket stuff called 'Ignition!' by John Clark, that's a really fun one." — Elon Musk

9. **Superintelligence: Paths, Dangers, Strategies by Nick Bostrom**

"Worth reading 'Superintelligence' by Bostrom. We need to be super careful with AI. Potentially more dangerous than nukes." — Elon Musk

10. **Zero to One: Notes on Startups, or How to Build the Future by Peter Thiel**

"Peter Thiel has built multiple breakthrough companies, and 'Zero to One' shows how." — Elon Musk

11. **Merchants of Doubt by Naomi Orestes and Erik M. Conway**

"Worth reading 'Merchants of Doubt.' Same who tried to deny smoking deaths or denying climate change." — Elon Musk

12. **The Hitchhiker's Guide to the Galaxy by Douglas Adams**

    "It's quite positive, and it highlighted an important point, which is that a lot of times the question is harder than the answer. And if you can properly phrase the question, then the answer is the easy part." — Elon Musk

13. **The Moon Is a Harsh Mistress by Robert Heinlein**

14. **The Culture series by Iain M. Banks**

    "Reading 'The Culture' series by Banks. Compelling picture of a grand, semi-utopian galactic future. Hopefully not too optimistic about AI." — Elon Musk

15. **Our Final Invention by James Barrat**

    "While on the subject of AI risk, 'Our Final Invention' by James Barrat is also worth reading." — Elon Musk

16. **Life 3.0: Being Human in the Age of Artificial Intelligence by Max Tegmark**

    "Worth reading 'Life 3.0' by Tegmark. AI will be the best or worst thing ever for humanity, so let's get it right." — Elon Musk

17. **Stranger in a Strange Land by Robert A. Heinlein**

18. **Lord of the Flies by William Golding**

19. **Lying by Sam Harris**

    "Read 'Lying', the new book by my friend Sam Harris. Excellent cover art and lots of good reasons not to lie!" — Elon Musk

20. **The Lost Planet by Rachel Searles**

    "My kids love 'The Lost Planet' by Rachel Searles. Now on a rare second read!" — Elon Musk

Scan the QR Code to find more information for each book.

FREE book

For a limited time Olivia Longray is giving away the book called "A Simple Weight Loss Plan That Can Work for You: How to Lose Weight Quickly in an Atmosphere of Love."

This is your only chance to get it FREE (no strings attached).

Scan this QR code.

Enjoy!

Your Reviews

If the book proves useful and appealing to you, please, leave a short review on the book's Amazon page and give me your thoughts on it! Your opinion will surely help other readers to decide if my book is worth their time and money. Tell others of your impressions and my thanks to you for it in advance!

Have a great day!

Olivia Longray

A Note on Sources

1. "WGS17 Session: A Conversation with Elon Musk," World Government Summit, February 13, 2017, https://youtu.be/rCoFKUJ_8Y0

2. "Elon Musk's USC Commencement Speech | USC Marshall School of Business Undergraduate Commencement 2014," USC, 2014, https://youtu.be/e7Qh-vwpYH8

3. "WGS17 Session: A Conversation with Elon Musk," World Government Summit, February 13, 2017, https://youtu.be/rCoFKUJ_8Y0

4. "Driving With Elon Musk," Forbes Life, March, 2012, https://www.youtube.com/watch?v=VSNXhHTLLIk

5. "WGS17 Session: A Conversation with Elon Musk," World Government Summit, February 13, 2017, https://youtu.be/rCoFKUJ_8Y0

6. Kevin Daum, "Elon Musk's 40 Insights on Achieving True Greatness," Inc., July 21, 2016, https://www.inc.com/kevin-daum/elon-musk-s-40-insights-on-achieving-true-greatness.html

7. Thomas Ricker, "Elon Musk: We're already cyborgs," The Verge, June 2, 2016, https://www.theverge.com/2016/6/2/11837854/neural-lace-cyborgs-elon-musk

8. Kevin Daum, "Elon Musk's 40 Insights on Achieving True Greatness," Inc., July 21, 2016, https://www.inc.com/kevin-daum/elon-musk-s-40-insights-on-achieving-true-greatness.html

9. "WGS17 Session: A Conversation with Elon Musk," World Government Summit, February 13, 2017, https://youtu.be/rCoFKUJ_8Y0

10. "Elon Musk: The Architect of Tomorrow," Rolling Stone, November 15, 2017, https://www.rollingstone.com/culture/features/elon-musk-inventors-plans-for-outer-space-cars-finding-love-w511747

11. Matt Rosoff, "Elon Musk Worries That His Kids Are Too Soft To Be Entrepreneurs," Business Insider, September 16, 2011,

12. Tad Friend, "Plugged In: Can Elon Musk lead the way to an electric-car future?" The New Yorker, August 24, 2009, https://www.newyorker.com/magazine/2009/08/24/plugged-in
13. "Elon Musk: The Architect of Tomorrow," Rolling Stone, November 15, 2017, https://www.rollingstone.com/culture/features/elon-musk-inventors-plans-for-outer-space-cars-finding-love-w511747
14. Kevin Daum, "Elon Musk's 40 Insights on Achieving True Greatness," Inc., July 21, 2016, https://www.inc.com/kevin-daum/elon-musk-s-40-insights-on-achieving-true-greatness.html
15. "Elon Musk: How I Became The Real 'Iron Man'," Bloomberg, June 10, 2014, https://youtu.be/mh45igK4Esw
16. "Elon Musk and the frontier of Technology," PBS: Think Tank, December 2007, http://www.pbs.org
17. "Interview With Elon Musk," Wired Science, PBS, January, 2007, https://www.youtube.com/watch?feature=player_embedded&v=Onajosm9PWo
18. "Elon Musk – Visionaries on Innovation," The Henry Ford, 2008, https://www.thehenryford.org/explore/stories-of-innovation/visionaries/elon-musk/
19. "Elon Musk Created Own School For His 5 Kids," Philosophy Workout, April, 2015, https://youtu.be/STt0dpgn900
20. "Elon Musk Profiled: Bloomberg Risk Takers," August 3, 2011, Bloomberg, https://www.bloomberg.com/quicktake/elon-musk
21. "Elon Musk: The Architect of Tomorrow," Rolling Stone, November 15, 2017, https://www.rollingstone.com/culture/features/elon-musk-inventors-plans-for-outer-space-cars-finding-love-w511747
22. "Elon Musk Profiled: Bloomberg Risk Takers," August 3, 2011, Bloomberg, https://www.bloomberg.com/quicktake/elon-musk

23. "Foundation 20 // Elon Musk," Kevin Rose, YouTube, September, 2012, https://youtu.be/L-s_3b5fRd8

24. "Space Mining vs. Human Space Flight," Stanford eCorner, 2003, http://ecorner.stanford.edu/videos/394/Space-Mining-vs-Human-Space-Flight

25. Alaina Levine, "Elon Musk on Mass, Mars, and MBAs," APS News, November 2013 (Volume 22, Number 10), http://www.aps.org/publications/apsnews/201311/profiles.cfm

26. The Joe Rogan Experience, REV, May 7, 2020, https://www.rev.com/blog/transcripts/joe-rogan-elon-musk-podcast-transcript-may-7-2020

27. "Elon Musk – Visionaries on Innovation," The Henry Ford, 2008, https://www.thehenryford.org/explore/stories-of-innovation/visionaries/elon-musk/

28. Carl Hoffman, "Elon Musk, the Rocket Man With a Sweet Ride," Smithsonian Magazine, December, 2012, http://www.smithsonianmag.com/science-nature/elon-musk-the-rocket-man-with-a-sweet-ride-136059680/

29. Matt McFarland, "When Elon Musk lived on $1 a day," The Washington Post, March 24, 2015, https://www.washingtonpost.com/news/innovations/wp/2015/03/24/when-elon-musk-lived-on-1-a-day/

30. "Opportunities in Space: Mars Oasis," Stanford eCorner, October 8, 2003, http://ecorner.stanford.edu/videos/381/

31. 11 Elon Musk Quotes That Show His Genius, Business Insider, September 12, 2013, http://www.businessinsider.in/tech/11-elon-musk-quotes-that-show-his-genius/slidelist/22503747.cms

32. "Too Crazy To Be Lucky: A Chat With Elon Musk," Startups.co, November 28, 2016, https://www.startups.co/articles/too-crazy-to-be-lucky

33. "The mind behind Tesla, SpaceX, SolarCity...," TED Talks, February, 2013, https://www.ted.com/talks/elon_musk_the_mind_behind_tesla_spacex_solarcity

34. Jack Delosa, "The making of Tesla's Elon Musk," Financial Review, April 15, 2016, http://www.afr.com/leadership/the-making-of-elon-musk-20160415-go71vb

35. "Elon Musk: Correcting The Record About My Divorce," Business Insider, July 8, 2010, http://www.businessinsider.com/correcting-the-record-about-my-divorce-2010-7

36. "WGS17 Session: A Conversation with Elon Musk," World Government Summit, February 13, 2017, https://youtu.be/rCoFKUJ_8Yo

37. Elon Musk: The Architect of Tomorrow," Rolling Stone, November 15, 2017, https://www.rollingstone.com/culture/features/elon-musk-inventors-plans-for-outer-space-cars-finding-love-w511747

38. Ashlee Vance, Elon Musk: Tesla, SpaceX and the Quest for a Fantastic Future, 2015

39. "Elon Musk: The Architect of Tomorrow," Rolling Stone, November 15, 2017, https://www.rollingstone.com/culture/features/elon-musk-inventors-plans-for-outer-space-cars-finding-love-w511747

40. The Joe Rogan Experience, REV, May 7, 2020, https://www.rev.com/blog/transcripts/joe-rogan-elon-musk-podcast-transcript-may-7-2020

41. Elon Musk, Twitter, July 25, 2017, https://twitter.com/elonmusk/status/889736220116254721

42. Carl Hoffman, "Elon Musk, the Rocket Man With a Sweet Ride," Smithsonian Magazine, December, 2012, http://www.smithsonianmag.com/science-nature/elon-musk-the-rocket-man-with-a-sweet-ride-136059680/

43. Kevin Daum, "Elon Musk's 40 Insights on Achieving True Greatness," Inc., July 21, 2016, https://www.inc.com/kevin-daum/elon-musk-s-40-insights-on-achieving-true-greatness.html

44. "Too Crazy To Be Lucky: A Chat With Elon Musk," Startups.co, November 28, 2016, https://www.startups.co/articles/too-crazy-to-be-lucky

45. "Elon Musk: The Architect of Tomorrow," Rolling Stone, November 15, 2017, https://www.rollingstone.com/culture/features/elon-musk-inventors-plans-for-outer-space-cars-finding-love-w511747

46. Mike Isaac, "Elon Musk Talks About His Falling Out With the ZuckerPAC," All Things Digital, May 29, 2013, http://allthingsd.com/20130529/elon-musk-talks-about-his-falling-out-with-the-zuckerpac/

47. Danielle Muoio, "The 13 craziest things Elon Musk believes right now," Business Insider, October 25, 2016, http://www.businessinsider.com/13-crazy-elon-musk-quotes-things-he-believes-2016-10/

48. "The future we're building – and boring," TED Talks, April, 2017, https://youtu.be/zIwLWfaAg-8

49. "Elon Musk – Visionaries on Innovation," The Henry Ford, 2008, https://www.thehenryford.org/explore/stories-of-innovation/visionaries/elon-musk/

50. Ashlee Vance, Elon Musk: Tesla, SpaceX and the Quest for a Fantastic Future, 2015

51. Ian O'Neill, "Elon Musk: "I Will Never Give Up" after Falcon 1 loss," Universe Today, December 24, 2015, https://www.universetoday.com/16440/elon-musk-i-will-never-give-up-after-falcon-1-loss/

52. "Too Crazy To Be Lucky: A Chat With Elon Musk," Startups.co, November 28, 2016, https://www.startups.co/articles/too-crazy-to-be-lucky

53. Chris Green, "Elon Musk: It's Always the Quiet Ones," The Independent, June 7, 2014, https://www.independent.co.uk/life-style/gadgets-and-tech/elon-musk-its-always-the-quiet-ones-9506963.html

54. Marlow Stern, "Elon Musk of Tesla Motors Discusses Revenge of the Electric Car," Daily Beast, April 25, 2011, http://www.thedailybeast.com/elon-musk-of-tesla-motors-discusses-revenge-of-the-electric-car

55. Tom Junod, "Elon Musk: Triumph of His Will," Esquire, November 14, 2012, http://www.esquire.com/news-politics/a16681/elon-musk-interview-1212/

56. "Opportunities in Space: Mars Oasis," Stanford eCorner, 2003, http://ecorner.stanford.edu/videos/381/
57. "The future we're building – and boring," TED Talks, April, 2017, https://youtu.be/zIwLWfaAg-8
58. Elon Musk, Twitter, December 2, 2017, https://twitter.com/elonmusk/status/937041986304983040
59. "The future we're building – and boring," TED Talks, April, 2017, https://youtu.be/zIwLWfaAg-8
60. Sebastian Blanco, "Tesla Supercharger network goes nationwide, gets quicker," Autoblog, May 30, 2013, https://www.autoblog.com
61. "Too Crazy To Be Lucky: A Chat With Elon Musk," Startups.co, November 28, 2016, https://www.startups.co/articles/too-crazy-to-be-lucky
62. "Elon Musk Interview with Charlie Rose," CharlieRose.com, August 11, 2009, https://charlierose.com/videos/12550
63. GQ Magazine, 2013, http://www.gq-magazine.co.uk
64. "The future we're building – and boring," TED Talks, April, 2017, https://youtu.be/zIwLWfaAg-8
65. Anthony Ffrench-Constant, "Elon Musk talks Tesla," GQ, November 26, 2014, http://www.gq-magazine.co.uk/article/elon-musk-interview-tesla-p85d-mars
66. Elon Musk, Twitter, August 02, 2017, https://twitter.com/elonmusk/status/892545286748258305
67. David Ly Khim, "6 Life-Changing Lessons, Advice, & Tips From Elon Musk," HubSpot, October 05, 2017, https://blog.hubspot.com/sales/lessons-from-elon-musk
68. "Elon Musk: The Architect of Tomorrow," Rolling Stone, November 15, 2017, https://www.rollingstone.com/culture/features/elon-musk-inventors-plans-for-outer-space-cars-finding-love-w511747
69. SpaceX careers page, http://www.spacex.com/careers

70. "Elon Musk: How to Build the Future," Y Combinator, September, 2016, https://youtu.be/tnBQmEqBCY0

71. "Space X Heralds New Era of Travel," Engineering.com, 2012, http://www.engineering.com/Videos/LearningSeriesChannel/VideoId/2952/Space-X-Heralds-New-Era-Of-Travel.aspx

72. Tom Junod, "Elon Musk: Triumph of His Will," Esquire, November 14, 2012, http://www.esquire.com/news-politics/a16681/elon-musk-interview-1212/

73. "Elon Musk – Visionaries on Innovation," The Henry Ford, 2008, https://www.thehenryford.org/explore/stories-of-innovation/visionaries/elon-musk/

74. "The future we're building – and boring," TED Talks, April, 2017, https://youtu.be/zIwLWfaAg-8

75. "The future we're building – and boring," TED Talks, April 2017, https://youtu.be/zIwLWfaAg-8

76. "Elon Musk – the Future of Energy & Transport," Oxford Martin School, 2012, https://youtu.be/c1HZIQliuoA

77. "The mind behind Tesla, SpaceX, SolarCity…," TED Talks, February, 2013, https://www.ted.com/talks/elon_musk_the_mind_behind_tesla_spacex_solarcity

78. "The mind behind Tesla, SpaceX, SolarCity…," TED Talks, February, 2013, https://www.ted.com/talks/elon_musk_the_mind_behind_tesla_spacex_solarcity

79. "WGS17 Session: A Conversation with Elon Musk," World Government Summit, February 13, 2017, https://youtu.be/rCoFKUJ_8Y0

80. Danielle Muoio, "The 13 craziest things Elon Musk believes right now," Business Insider, October 25, 2016, http://www.businessinsider.com/13-crazy-elon-musk-quotes-things-he-believes-2016-10/

81. "The future we're building – and boring," TED Talks, April, 2017, https://youtu.be/zIwLWfaAg-8

82. "GTC 2015 Opening Keynote with Jen-Hsun Huang, NVIDIA," GPU Technology Conference, 2015, http://www.ustream.tv/recorded/60025825
83. "The future we're building – and boring," TED Talks, April, 2017, https://youtu.be/zIwLWfaAg-8
84. "The future we're building – and boring," TED Talks, April, 2017, https://youtu.be/zIwLWfaAg-8
85. "WGS17 Session: A Conversation with Elon Musk," World Government Summit, February 13, 2017, https://youtu.be/rCoFKUJ_8Yo
86. Elon Musk, Instagram, August 04, 2017, https://www.instagram.com/p/BXXiVWFgphb/
87. "Elon Musk | SXSW Live 2013 | SXSW ON," SXSW, March 9, 2013, https://youtu.be/LeQMWdOMa-A
88. "Elon Musk – Visionaries on Innovation," The Henry Ford, 2008, https://www.thehenryford.org/explore/stories-of-innovation/visionaries/elon-musk/
89. Rory Carroll, "Elon Musk's mission to Mars," The Guardian, July 17, 2013, https://www.theguardian.com/technology/2013/jul/17/elon-musk-mission-mars-spacex
90. "Elon Musk: How to Build the Future," Y Combinator, September, 2016, https://youtu.be/tnBQmEqBCYo
91. Danielle Muoio, "The 13 craziest things Elon Musk believes right now," Business Insider, October 25, 2016, http://www.businessinsider.com/13-crazy-elon-musk-quotes-things-he-believes-2016-10/
92. "One-on-one with Elon Musk," MIT Centennial Symposium, AeroAstroMIT, October 24, 2014, https://www.youtube.com/watch?v=PULkWGHeIQQ
93. Danielle Muoio, "The 13 craziest things Elon Musk believes right now," Business Insider, October 25, 2016, http://www.businessinsider.com/13-crazy-elon-musk-quotes-things-he-believes-2016-10/
94. "WGS17 Session: A Conversation with Elon Musk," World Government Summit, February 13, 2017, https://youtu.be/rCoFKUJ_8Yo

95. Robert Strauss, "The Next, Next Thing," The Pennsylvania Gazette, November 4, 2008, http://www.upenn.edu/gazette/1108/feature4_1.html

96. Joey Roulette, "SpaceX's Falcon Heavy rocket soars in debut test launch from Florida", Reuters, February 6, 2018, https://www.reuters.com/article/us-space-spacex-heavy/spacexs-falcon-heavy-rocket-soars-in-debut-test-launch-from-florida-idUSKBN1FQ1HZ

97. Tom Junod, "Elon Musk: Triumph of His Will," Esquire, November 14, 2012, http://www.esquire.com/news-politics/a16681/elon-musk-interview-1212/

98. "The mind behind Tesla, SpaceX, SolarCity…," TED Talks, February, 2013, https://www.ted.com/talks/elon_musk_the_mind_behind_tesla_spacex_solarcity

99. "The future we're building – and boring," TED Talks, April, 2017, https://youtu.be/zIwLWfaAg-8

100. "The mind behind Tesla, SpaceX, SolarCity…," TED Talks, February, 2013, https://www.ted.com/talks/elon_musk_the_mind_behind_tesla_spacex_solarcity

101. "The future we're building – and boring," TED Talks, April, 2017, https://youtu.be/zIwLWfaAg-8

102. Kevin Daum, "Elon Musk's 40 Insights on Achieving True Greatness," Inc., July 21, 2016, https://www.inc.com/kevin-daum/elon-musk-s-40-insights-on-achieving-true-greatness.html

103. Mohit Bansal Chandigarh, "Some Quotes By Elon Musk That Will Motivate You To Follow Your Dreams," YourStory, August 20, 2019, https://yourstory.com/mystory/some-quotes-by-elon-musk-that-will-motivate-you-to

104. Megan Garber, "The Real iPod: Elon Musk's Wild Idea for a 'Jetson Tunnel' from S.F. to L.A.," The Atlantic, July 21, 2012, https://www.theatlantic.com/technology/archive/2012/07/the-real-ipod-elon-musks-wild-idea-for-a-jetson-tunnel-from-sf-to-la/259825/

105. Biz Carson, "15 brilliant or just plain crazy quotes from eccentric billionaire Elon Musk," Business Insider, June 4, 2016, http://www.businessinsider.com/15-crazy-and-brilliant-elon-musk-quotes-2016-6/

106. "WGS17 Session: A Conversation with Elon Musk," World Government Summit, February 13, 2017, https://youtu.be/rCoFKUJ_8Yo

107. "The future we're building – and boring," TED Talks, April, 2017, https://youtu.be/zIwLWfaAg-8

108. "WGS17 Session: A Conversation with Elon Musk," World Government Summit, February 13, 2017, https://youtu.be/rCoFKUJ_8Yo

109. Elon Musk, Twitter, August 12, 2017, https://twitter.com/elonmusk/status/896166762361704450

110. "Elon Musk: How to Build the Future," Y Combinator, September, 2016, https://youtu.be/tnBQmEqBCY0

111. Danielle Muoio, "The 13 craziest things Elon Musk believes right now," Business Insider, October 25, 2016, http://www.businessinsider.com/13-crazy-elon-musk-quotes-things-he-believes-2016-10/

112. "Elon Musk: How to Build the Future," Y Combinator, September, 2016, https://youtu.be/tnBQmEqBCY0

113. The Joe Rogan Experience, REV, May 7, 2020, https://www.rev.com/blog/transcripts/joe-rogan-elon-musk-podcast-transcript-may-7-2020

114. Danielle Muoio, "The 13 craziest things Elon Musk believes right now," Business Insider, October 25, 2016, http://www.businessinsider.com/13-crazy-elon-musk-quotes-things-he-believes-2016-10/

115. Stephen Shankland, Jackson Ryan, "Elon Musk shows Neuralink brain implant working in a pig," CNET.com, August 29, 2020, https://www.cnet.com/news/elon-musk-shows-neuralink-brain-implant-working-in-a-pig/

116. The Joe Rogan Experience, REV, May 7, 2020, https://www.rev.com/blog/transcripts/joe-rogan-elon-musk-podcast-transcript-may-7-2020

117. "Elon Musk – the Future of Energy & Transport," Oxford Martin School, 2012, https://youtu.be/c1HZIQliu0A

118. "Elon Musk: The Architect of Tomorrow," Rolling Stone, November 15, 2017, https://www.rollingstone.com/culture/features/elon-musk-inventors-plans-for-outer-space-cars-finding-love-w511747

119. Danielle Muoio, "The 13 craziest things Elon Musk believes right now," Business Insider, October 25, 2016, http://www.businessinsider.com/13-crazy-elon-musk-quotes-things-he-believes-2016-10/

120. Danielle Muoio, "The 13 craziest things Elon Musk believes right now," Business Insider, October 25, 2016, http://www.businessinsider.com/13-crazy-elon-musk-quotes-things-he-believes-2016-10/

121. "WGS17 Session: A Conversation with Elon Musk," World Government Summit, February 13, 2017, https://youtu.be/rCoFKUJ_8Y0

122. Biz Carson, "15 brilliant or just plain crazy quotes from eccentric billionaire Elon Musk," Business Insider, June 4, 2016, http://www.businessinsider.com/15-crazy-and-brilliant-elon-musk-quotes-2016-6/

123. Elon Musk, Twitter, June 26, 2020, https://twitter.com/elonmusk/status/1276418907968925696?fbclid

124. The Economic Club of Chicago, April 2012, https://www.econclubchi.org/

125. Kevin Daum, "Elon Musk's 40 Insights on Achieving True Greatness," Inc., July 21, 2016, https://www.inc.com/kevin-daum/elon-musk-s-40-insights-on-achieving-true-greatness.html

126. "Elon Musk: How to Build the Future," Y Combinator, September, 2016, https://youtu.be/tnBQmEqBCY0

127. "Elon Musk – Visionaries on Innovation," The Henry Ford, 2008, https://www.thehenryford.org/explore/stories-of-innovation/visionaries/elon-musk/

128. Kevin Daum, "Elon Musk's 40 Insights on Achieving True Greatness," Inc., July 21, 2016, https://www.inc.com/kevin-

129. Kevin Daum, "Elon Musk's 40 Insights on Achieving True Greatness," Inc., July 21, 2016, https://www.inc.com/kevin-daum/elon-musk-s-40-insights-on-achieving-true-greatness.html

130. "11 Elon Musk Quotes That Show His Genius," Business Insider, September 12, 2013, http://www.businessinsider.in/tech/11-elon-musk-quotes-that-show-his-genius/slidelist/22503747.cms

131. "Elon Musk Captured by Rainn Wilson! | Metaphysical Milkshake," SoulPancake, March 18, 2013, https://youtu.be/NsoIHCj2q-E

132. "Opportunities in Space: Mars Oasis," Stanford eCorner, October 8, 2003, http://ecorner.stanford.edu/videos/381/

133. "Christopher Kai Interviews Billionaire Elon Musk," Christopher Kai, March, 2014, https://youtu.be/udYUyGCIV-8

134. Kevin Daum, "Elon Musk's 40 Insights on Achieving True Greatness," Inc., July 21, 2016, https://www.inc.com/kevin-daum/elon-musk-s-40-insights-on-achieving-true-greatness.html

135. "Elon Musk: How to Build the Future," Y Combinator, September, 2016, https://youtu.be/tnBQmEqBCY0

136. Kevin Daum, "Elon Musk's 40 Insights on Achieving True Greatness," Inc., July 21, 2016, https://www.inc.com/kevin-daum/elon-musk-s-40-insights-on-achieving-true-greatness.html

137. Kevin Daum, "Elon Musk's 40 Insights on Achieving True Greatness," Inc., July 21, 2016, https://www.inc.com/kevin-daum/elon-musk-s-40-insights-on-achieving-true-greatness.html

138. 11 Elon Musk Quotes That Show His Genius, Business Insider, September 12, 2013, http://www.businessinsider.in/tech/11-elon-musk-quotes-that-show-his-genius/slidelist/22503747.cms

139. "Elon Musk Hits Frontier Milestones With SpaceX, Tesla," Investor's Business Daily, August 21, 2012, http://www.investors.com/news/management/leaders-and-success/elon-musk-launched-spacex-tesla/

140. "Lessons on Leadership: Elon Musk + Sir Richard Branson," Google for Startups, August 8, 2013, https://youtu.be/Vy9y_YSpYxA

141. Robin Keats, "Rocket man by Robin Keats," Queen's Alumni Review, Issue #1, 2013, http://www.queensu.ca/gazette/alumnireview/stories/rocket-man

142. Robin Keats, "Rocket man by Robin Keats," Queen's Alumni Review, Issue #1, 2013, http://www.queensu.ca/gazette/alumnireview/stories/rocket-man

143. Kevin Daum, "Elon Musk's 40 Insights on Achieving True Greatness," Inc., July 21, 2016, https://www.inc.com/kevin-daum/elon-musk-s-40-insights-on-achieving-true-greatness.html

144. Kevin Daum, "Elon Musk's 40 Insights on Achieving True Greatness," Inc., July 21, 2016, https://www.inc.com/kevin-daum/elon-musk-s-40-insights-on-achieving-true-greatness.html

145. "Elon Musk - Visionaries on Innovation," The Henry Ford, 2008, https://www.thehenryford.org/explore/stories-of-innovation/visionaries/elon-musk/

146. "The future we're building – and boring," TED Talks, April, 2017, https://youtu.be/zIwLWfaAg-8

147. Carl Hoffman, "Now 0-for-3, SpaceX's Elon Musk Vows to Make Orbit," Wired, August 5, 2008, http://www.wired.com/science/space/news/2008/08/musk_qa

148. Larry Kim, "50 Innovation and Success Quotes from SpaceX Founder Elon Musk," Inc., March 8, 2016, https://www.inc.com/larry-kim/50-innovation-amp;-success-quotes-from-spacex-founder-elon-musk.html

149. "Elon Musk Might Be A Super Villain," The Late Show with Stephen Colbert, 2015, https://youtu.be/gV6hP9wpMW8

150. "The mind behind Tesla, SpaceX, SolarCity...," TED Talks, February, 2013, https://www.ted.com/talks/elon_musk_the_mind_behind_tesla_spacex_solarcity

151. "Elon Musk Profiled: Bloomberg Risk Takers," August 3, 2011, Bloomberg, https://www.bloomberg.com/quicktake/elon-musk

152. Kevin Daum, "Elon Musk's 40 Insights on Achieving True Greatness," Inc., July 21, 2016, https://www.inc.com/kevin-daum/elon-musk-s-40-insights-on-achieving-true-greatness.html

153. "Elon Musk interviewed on Danish TV, 27th September 2015," Inspired Action, 2017, https://www.youtube.com/watch?v=rdCkDSXQC1Q

154. "CHM Revolutionaries: An Evening with Elon Musk," Computer History Museum, 2013, https://youtu.be/AHHwXUm3iIg

155. Andrew Corsello, "The Believer," GQ Magazine, December 31, 2008, http://www.gq.com/news-politics/newsmakers/200901/elon-musk-paypal-solar-power-electric-cars-space-travel

156. Sebastian Blanco, "In deep with Tesla CEO Elon Musk: Financials, Falcon doors and finding faults in the Model S," Autoblog, September 7, 2012, https://www.autoblog.com/2012/09/07/tesla-ceo-elon-musk-q-and-a/

157. "WGS17 Session: A Conversation with Elon Musk," World Government Summit, February 13, 2017, https://youtu.be/rCoFKUJ_8Yo

158. "Elon Musk | SXSW Live 2013 | SXSW ON," SXSW, March 9, 2013, https://youtu.be/LeQMWdOMa-A

159. Matt Rosoff, "Elon Musk Worries That His Kids Are Too Soft To Be Entrepreneurs," Business Insider, September 16, 2011, http://www.businessinsider.com/elon-musk-worries-that-his-kids-are-too-soft-to-be-entrepreneurs-2011-9

160. "Elon Musk: How to Build the Future," Y Combinator, September, 2016, https://youtu.be/tnBQmEqBCY0

161. "Elon Musk: How to Build the Future," Y Combinator, September, 2016, https://youtu.be/tnBQmEqBCY0

162. "Elon Musk - Visionaries on Innovation," The Henry Ford, 2008, https://www.thehenryford.org/explore/stories-of-innovation/visionaries/elon-musk/

163. "WGS17 Session: A Conversation with Elon Musk," World Government Summit, February 13, 2017, https://youtu.be/rCoFKUJ_8Y0

164. "The mind behind Tesla, SpaceX, SolarCity…," TED Talks, February, 2013, https://www.ted.com/talks/elon_musk_the_mind_behind_tesla_spacex_solarcity

165. "Elon Musk: New York Times Likely Cost Tesla Hundreds of Orders," Bloomberg, February, 2013, https://youtu.be/dg04f_nGlz0

166. "Elon Musk: The Architect of Tomorrow," Rolling Stone, November 15, 2017, https://www.rollingstone.com/culture/features/elon-musk-inventors-plans-for-outer-space-cars-finding-love-w511747

167. Kevin Daum, "Elon Musk's 40 Insights on Achieving True Greatness," Inc., July 21, 2016, https://www.inc.com/kevin-daum/elon-musk-s-40-insights-on-achieving-true-greatness.html

168. "Elon Musk USC Commencement Speech | USC Marshall School of Business Undergraduate Commencement 2014," USC, 2014, https://youtu.be/e7Qh-vwpYH8

169. Jana Kasperkevic, "Elon Musk and Richard Branson's Best Advice for Entrepreneurs," Inc., August 08, 2013, https://www.inc.com/jana-kasperkevic/google-hangout-advice-elon-musk-richard-branson.html

170. "Elon Musk – CEO of Tesla Motors and SpaceX | Entrepreneurship |," Khan Academy, 2013, https://youtu.be/vDwzmJpI4io

171. Kevin Daum, "Elon Musk's 40 Insights on Achieving True Greatness," Inc., July 21, 2016, https://www.inc.com/kevin-daum/elon-musk-s-40-insights-on-achieving-true-greatness.html

172. Kevin Daum, "Elon Musk's 40 Insights on Achieving True Greatness," Inc., July 21, 2016, https://www.inc.com/kevin-daum/elon-musk-s-40-insights-on-achieving-true-greatness.html

173. "Elon Musk - CEO of Tesla Motors and SpaceX | Entrepreneurship |," Khan Academy, April 17, 2013, https://youtu.be/vDwzmJpI4io

174. Kevin Daum, "Elon Musk's 40 Insights on Achieving True Greatness," Inc., July 21, 2016, https://www.inc.com/kevin-daum/elon-musk-s-40-insights-on-achieving-true-greatness.html

175. "Elon Musk USC Commencement Speech | USC Marshall School of Business Undergraduate Commencement 2014," USC, 2014, https://youtu.be/e7Qh-vwpYH8

176. Kevin Daum, "Elon Musk's 40 Insights on Achieving True Greatness," Inc., July 21, 2016, https://www.inc.com/kevin-daum/elon-musk-s-40-insights-on-achieving-true-greatness.html

177. Kevin Daum, "Elon Musk's 40 Insights on Achieving True Greatness," Inc., July 21, 2016, https://www.inc.com/kevin-daum/elon-musk-s-40-insights-on-achieving-true-greatness.html

178. Larry Kim, "50 Innovation and Success Quotes from SpaceX Founder Elon Musk," Inc., March 8, 2016, https://www.inc.com/larry-kim/50-innovation-amp;-success-quotes-from-spacex-founder-elon-musk.html

179. "Opportunities in Space: Mars Oasis," Stanford eCorner, October 8, 2003, http://ecorner.stanford.edu/videos/381/

180. Kevin Daum, "Elon Musk's 40 Insights on Achieving True Greatness," Inc., July 21, 2016, https://www.inc.com/kevin-daum/elon-musk-s-40-insights-on-achieving-true-greatness.html

181. Kevin Daum, "Elon Musk's 40 Insights on Achieving True Greatness," Inc., July 21, 2016, https://www.inc.com/kevin-daum/elon-musk-s-40-insights-on-achieving-true-greatness.html

182. Kamelia Angelova, "How Elon Musk Can Tell If Job Applicants Are Lying About Their Experience," Business

Insider, December 26, 2013, http://www.businessinsider.com/elon-musk-job-interview-rule-2013-12

183. Nathan Furr, "Why Innovators Hate M.B.A.'s," Inc., September 19, 2014, https://www.inc.com/nathan-furr/why-innovators-hate-mbas.html

184. Kevin Daum, "Elon Musk's 40 Insights on Achieving True Greatness," Inc., July 21, 2016, https://www.inc.com/kevin-daum/elon-musk-s-40-insights-on-achieving-true-greatness.html

185. "What Elon Musk Taught Me About Growing A Business, HubSpot, October, 2017, https://www.youtube.com/watch?v=i0yqJa48ebs

186. Kevin Daum, "Elon Musk's 40 Insights on Achieving True Greatness," Inc., July 21, 2016, https://www.inc.com/kevin-daum/elon-musk-s-40-insights-on-achieving-true-greatness.html

187. Kevin Daum, "Elon Musk's 40 Insights on Achieving True Greatness," Inc., July 21, 2016, https://www.inc.com/kevin-daum/elon-musk-s-40-insights-on-achieving-true-greatness.html

188. "Tesla Motors, Inc. 2013 annual shareholder meeting," Tesla Schweiz (Community Channel), June 4, 2013, https://youtu.be/n3AcKTma0E8

189. Kevin Daum, "Elon Musk's 40 Insights on Achieving True Greatness," Inc., July 21, 2016, https://www.inc.com/kevin-daum/elon-musk-s-40-insights-on-achieving-true-greatness.html

190. "Opportunities in Space: Mars Oasis," Stanford eCorner, October 8, 2003, http://ecorner.stanford.edu/videos/381/

191. "The mind behind Tesla, SpaceX, SolarCity...," TED Talks, February, 2013, https://www.ted.com/talks/elon_musk_the_mind_behind_tesla_spacex_solarcity

192. Elon Musk, "All Our Patent Are Belong To You," June 12, 2014, https://www.tesla.com/blog/all-our-patent-are-belong-you

193. Kevin Daum, "Elon Musk's 40 Insights on Achieving True Greatness," Inc., July 21, 2016, https://www.inc.com/kevin-daum/elon-musk-s-40-insights-on-achieving-true-greatness.html

194. "Opportunities in Space: Mars Oasis," Stanford eCorner, October 8, 2003, http://ecorner.stanford.edu/videos/381/

195. "Elon Musk: The Architect of Tomorrow," Rolling Stone, November 15, 2017, https://www.rollingstone.com/culture/features/elon-musk-inventors-plans-for-outer-space-cars-finding-love-w511747

196. "Elon Musk – Visionaries on Innovation," The Henry Ford, 2008, https://www.thehenryford.org/explore/stories-of-innovation/visionaries/elon-musk/

197. Kevin Daum, "Elon Musk's 40 Insights on Achieving True Greatness," Inc., July 21, 2016, https://www.inc.com/kevin-daum/elon-musk-s-40-insights-on-achieving-true-greatness.html

198. "Elon Musk: 3 Secrets of my Success," FUSE, June 29, 2011, https://info.fusefinancialpartners.com/blog/elon_musk_interview

199. Kevin Daum, "Elon Musk's 40 Insights on Achieving True Greatness," Inc., July 21, 2016, https://www.inc.com/kevin-daum/elon-musk-s-40-insights-on-achieving-true-greatness.html

Follow me on social media:

https://twitter.com/olivia_longray
https://facebook.com/olivia.longray
https://instagram.com/olivia_longray

Printed in Great Britain
by Amazon